GRAPHING CALCULATOR MANUAL

to accompany

PRECALCULUS
FUNCTIONS AND GRAPHS
FIFTH EDITION
AND
PRECALCULUS
GRAPHICAL, NUMERICAL, ALGEBRAIC
SIXTH EDITION

FRANKLIN DEMANA
Ohio State University
BERT K. WAITS
Ohio State University
GREGORY D. FOLEY
Appalachian State University
DANIEL KENNEDY
Baylor School

PEARSON
Addison
Wesley

Boston   San Francisco   New York
London   Toronto   Sydney   Tokyo   Singapore   Madrid
Mexico City   Munich   Paris   Cape Town   Hong Kong   Montreal

Reproduced by Pearson Addison-Wesley from electronic files supplied by Laurel Technical Services.

Copyright © 2004 Pearson Education, Inc.

ISBN   0-321-13199-1
  3 4 5 6 VHG 06 05

Table of Contents

Chapter 1: Grapher Workshop   1

Chapter 2: TI-82, TI-83, and TI-83 Plus Graphing Calculators   25

Answers: Grapher Workshop   47

1

Grapher Workshop

1.1 Introduction

We call this chapter a workshop to emphasize that learning the grapher requires active hands-on work. In thousands of workshop hours over the past 10 years we have helped mathematics students and instructors learn how to use hand-held graphing calculators. Our reward has been the enthusiasm and excitement of the participants as they catch on to the remarkable way that a grapher aids their learning and teaching.

As much as we would like to do it, we cannot bring the actual workshop to you. Nevertheless, with some basic knowledge and your own creativity, you can learn to use and appreciate this technology. A few hours of productive play with this powerful tool will allow you to solve mathematical problems in new ways. As you read the text, you should work through the activities and examples using your grapher. Feel free to explore its menus and features. We suggest that you refer to this workshop whenever you encounter mathematics that require you to use features of the grapher that you are unfamiliar with. The grapher is a powerful tool. With play, thought, and practice, many students have found it both useful and exciting.

1.2 Numerical Computation and Editing

First Steps

Take a moment to study the keyboard of your grapher. The keys are grouped in "zones" according to their function: scientific calculation, graphing, editing, and various menus. Locate [ON]. Not only is it used to turn on your grapher, but it also acts as an [OFF] button as its *second function*, [2nd] [ON].

- Practice turning your calculator on and off.

Next determine how to adjust the screen contrast, something you may need to do as lighting conditions change or battery power weakens. (You may have to check your grapher owner's manual to see how this is done.)

- Adjust your screen contrast to make the screen very dark, then very light, and finally to suit your taste.

Grapher Notes: *In this workshop, boxed items in small caps, such as* $\boxed{\text{TAN}}$*, suggest grapher keys. Unboxed words in small caps, such as* FUNCTION MODE*, suggest on-screen menu items. Most grapher keys have multiple functions. You can access the second function of a key by first pressing the special colored* $\boxed{\text{2nd}}$ *or* $\boxed{\text{SHIFT}}$ *and its alphabetic function by pressing* $\boxed{\text{ALPHA}}$*.*

Performing Calculations

Computation is done on the *Home screen.*

- Try the calculations shown in Figure 1.1. Simply key in each expression, followed by $\boxed{\text{ENTER}}$ (or $\boxed{\text{EXE}}$). To find the value of log 100, use $\boxed{\text{LOG}}$. Do not enter the individual letters L, O, and G.

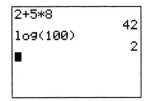

Figure 1.1

Error Messages

Don't be afraid to make a mistake! Just as pencils have erasers, graphers have delete ($\boxed{\text{DEL}}$) keys. Let's purposely make a mistake to see what happens.

- Key in 7 $\boxed{\div}$ 0, press $\boxed{\text{ENTER}}$, and observe your grapher's error message.

Error messages vary from grapher to grapher. Take a moment to read your grapher's error message. If a menu appears with a GoTo option, choose this option to "go to" the source of the error.

- Use your cursor keys ($\boxed{\blacktriangleleft}$, $\boxed{\blacktriangleright}$, $\boxed{\blacktriangle}$, and $\boxed{\blacktriangledown}$) and $\boxed{\text{DEL}}$ to change the expression from 7 ÷ 0 to 7 ÷ 2. Then enter this new expression.

Did you obtain the expected answer? If not, check your grapher owner's manual (CYGOM). (See the note below.) Take a few minutes to play with the editing features of your grapher. These few minutes could save you hours in the long run.

Grapher Note: *Keying sequences and other procedures vary somewhat from grapher to grapher, causing a need for you to "check your grapher owner's manual." We will abbreviate this instruction as* CYGOM.

Example 1   Replaying and Editing a Computation

If you deposit $500 in a savings account at a 4.5% interest rate, compounded annually, how much will you have in your account at the end of 2, 4, and 11 years?

Solution The total value S of the investment at the end of n years is

$$S = P(1 + r)^n,$$

where r is the interest rate. Because $4.5\% = 0.045, 1 + r = 1.045$.

- Enter the expression 500×1.045^2 on the Home screen of your grapher. If your answer has unwanted decimal places, change your *display mode* to two decimal places (CYGOM if necessary) and reenter the expression, as shown in Figure 1.2.

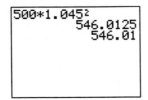

Figure 1.2 The compound interest expression computed in *floating point mode* and two decimal place *display mode*.

- *Replay* the previous entry. That is, reenter the expression without retyping the entire expression (CYGOM if necessary). Then change the exponent from 2 to 4. Repeat for the exponent 11, as shown in Figure 1.3.

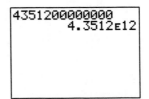

Figure 1.3 The compound interest expression computed for three different time values.

We conclude that the values in the account are $546.01 at the end of 2 years, $596.26 after 4 years, and $811.43 after 11 years.

Scientific Notation

The U.S. national debt as of 1993 was $4,351,200,000,000.

- Enter this number of dollars on the Home screen.

Your grapher will return the value in *scientific notation* because the number is so large. (See Figure 1.4.) We interpret this result as 4.3512×10^{12} dollars or, because 10^{12} is 1 trillion, as $4.3512 trillion.

Figure 1.4

The ANS Feature

When doing a series of calculations, you can easily use the answer from one calculation in the next calculation.

- Carry out the calculations shown in Figure 1.5 by pressing 7 [×] 7 [ENTER], then [×] 9 [ENTER], and finally [√‾] [ANS] [ENTER]. Note in the second step of the calculation that "Ans" automatically appeared on the screen because the grapher needed a quantity to multiply by 9.

Figure 1.5

When repeating a calculation recursively, you can use the ANS feature in an extremely useful way.

- Calculate a few terms of the geometric sequence that begins with 3 and grows by a constant factor of 5 by carrying out the calculation shown in Figure 1.6.

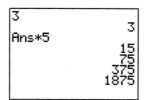

Figure 1.6

Using Variables

Another extremely helpful computational feature of the grapher is the ability to store and recall numbers as variables. The next activity illustrates using the variable x to evaluate a function at several different values of x. The activity also uses [:] to string together commands. If your grapher does not have [:], use [ENTER] instead.

- Evaluate $f(x) = x^2 + x - 2$ at $x = 1$ by pressing

$$1 \; \boxed{\text{STO}\blacktriangleright} \; \boxed{\text{X,T,}\theta} \; \boxed{:} \; \boxed{\text{X,T,}\theta} \; \boxed{x^2} \; \boxed{+} \; \boxed{\text{X,T,}\theta} \; \boxed{-} \; 2 \; \boxed{\text{ENTER}}.$$

Then use the replaying and editing features of your grapher to evaluate $f(6)$ and $f(-8)$, as shown in Figure 1.7.

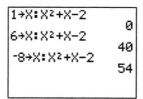

Figure 1.7

1.3   Table Building

A grapher feature even more powerful than the ability to store variables is the ability to store functions. This feature is the basis of graphing and table building. In either case the *Y= edit screen* is used to store the symbolic expressions (rules) for functions. A table can be used to evaluate a function for several different *x*-values.

- Press ⎡Y=⎤ (or [SYMB]) to go to the Y = screen. Then press ⎡X,T,θ⎤⎡x^2⎤⎡+⎤⎡X,T,θ⎤⎡−⎤ 2 ⎡ENTER⎤. See Figure 1.8a.

- Press ⎡TBLSET⎤ 0 ⎡ENTER⎤ 1 ⎡ENTER⎤⎡ENTER⎤. See Figure 1.8b. Then press ⎡TABLE⎤. See Figure 1.8c. (This key sequence will vary from grapher to grapher. CYGOM if necessary.)

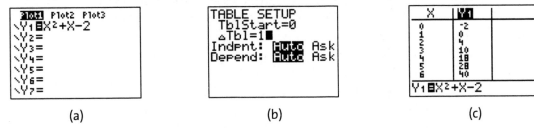

(a)	(b)	(c)

Figure 1.8 The steps in the table-building process on a grapher.

- Use the cursor keys (⎡►⎤, ⎡◄⎤, ⎡▲⎤, and ⎡▼⎤) to move around the table and explore. Pay attention to the readout at the bottom of the screen as you move to different "cells" in the table. What happens when you try to move the cursor off the top or bottom of the screen?

1.4   Function Graphing

Graphing and Exploring a Function

Most graphers have several graphing modes. Be sure that your grapher is in FUNCTION mode. The algebraic form for the function needs to be $f(x) = \ldots$, or $y = \ldots$.

Example 2   Graphing and Tracing along a Function

Use the FUNCTION mode to graph $f(x) = 2x + 1$. Explore the ordered pairs of the graph with the TRACE feature.

Solution   Figure 1.9 illustrates the procedure for graphing f in the window $[-6, 6]$ by $[-4, 4]$. Window is called range on some graphers.

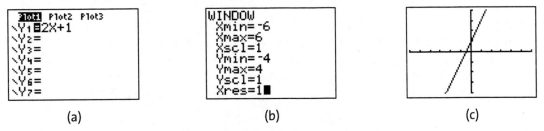

(a)	(b)	(c)

Figure 1.9 The steps in the graphing process.

- Enter $y = 2x + 1$ as shown in Figure 1.9a and the *window dimensions* as shown in Figure 1.9b. Then press ⎡GRAPH⎤ or [PLOT] to obtain the graph shown in Figure 1.9c.

- Press TRACE to display *x*- and *y*-coordinates of points on the graph. Use ▶ or ◀ to move from point to point. See Figure 1.10. This *tracing* shows you which points of $f(x) = 2x + 1$ were plotted by the grapher.

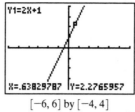

[−6, 6] by [−4, 4]

Figure 1.10 The graph of *f(x)* = 2*x* + 1 with the TRACE feature activated.

- Change the view dimensions to [−10, 10] by [−10, 10], known as the *standard window*. Some graphers have a ZOOM key. If yours does, press ZOOM, then choose ZSTANDARD from the menu to set the window to [−10, 10] by [−10, 10] automatically. Press TRACE and explore. Are the (*x, y*) pairs the same as you found using the window [−6, 6] by [−4, 4]?

A grapher allows you to obtain several views of the graph of a function. The Xmin and Xmax window dimensions determine which points the grapher plots and hence the coordinate readout when the TRACE feature is activated.

Your choice of Xmin and Xmax affects the *x*-coordinate readout when you trace along a graph. The reason is that the grapher screen is a rectangular array of *pixels,* short for "picture elements." The change in *x*-value that occurs when tracing is given by

$$\Delta x = \frac{\text{Xmax} - \text{Xmin}}{\text{Number of columns of pixels} - 1}.$$

The number of columns of pixels varies from grapher to grapher, as indicated in Table 1.1.

Table 1.1 The number of columns of pixels on various graphers

Grapher	Columns of Pixels
TI-80	63
Casio, Sharp, TI-82, TI-83	95
TI-81	96
TI-85	127
Hewlett-Packard	131
TI-92	239

FRIENDLY WINDOWS

As we observed in Example 2, the *x*-values displayed on the screen during tracing have many decimal places—for example, $x = 0.63829787$, as shown in Figure 1.10. Such "unfriendly" *x*-values can be avoided. You can use the [Xmin, Xmax] settings given in Table 1.2, or positive integer multiples of these settings, to guarantee a *friendly x*-coordinate readout when tracing. Windows with friendly *x*-coordinates are called *friendly windows.*

Table 1.2 The [Xmin, Xmax] dimensions for a basic friendly window on various graphers

Grapher	[Xmin, Xmax]
TI-80	[–3.1, 3.1]
Casio, Sharp, TI-82, TI-83	[–4.7, 4.7]
TI-81	[–4.8, 4.7]
TI-85	[–6.3, 6.3]
Hewlett-Packard	[–6.5, 6.5]
TI-92	[–11.9, 11.9]

Grapher Note: Some graphers have a ZDECIMAL *feature that sets* [Xmin, Xmax] *to the basic friendly settings and a* ZINTEGER *feature that can set the x-view dimensions to 10 times the basic friendly settings.*

- Graph the function $f(x) = 2x + 1$ from Example 2 in a friendly window, using the [Xmin, Xmax] settings given for your grapher in Table 1.2. Trace along the graph.
- Double the [Xmin, Xmax] and [Ymin, Ymax] settings and trace along the new view of the graph. How has the x-coordinate readout changed?
- Enter 10 times the settings given for your grapher in Table 1.2 to obtain *integer settings*. Trace to learn the reason for this name.

Square Windows

The graph of $f(x) = 2x + 1$ is a straight line with a slope of 2. You have seen several views of this graph in different windows. The apparent steepness of the graph can be quite different even though the slope is always 2.

- Graph $f(x) = 2x + 1$ in the window [–9, 9] by [–2, 2] and then in the window [–9, 9] by [–20, 20]. Compare the apparent steepness of the graph in the two windows.

In general, to obtain a graph that suggests the graph's true shape, you must choose viewing dimensions that are proportional to the dimensions of your grapher screen. Most grapher screens have a width-to-height ratio of roughly 3 : 2. Windows whose dimensions are proportional to the physical dimensions of the grapher screen are called *square windows*. Square windows yield true shapes: They make perpendicular lines look perpendicular, squares look square, and circles look circular.

Example 3 Rounding Out a Circle

Use your grapher to plot the circle $x^2 + y^2 = 1$.

Solution First, you will need to do some algebra:

$$x^2 + y^2 = 1$$
$$y^2 = 1 - x^2$$
$$y = \pm\sqrt{1 - x^2}$$

So the graph of the circle $x^2 + y^2 = 1$ is the union of the graphs of the functions $y_1 = \sqrt{1 - x^2}$ and $y_2 = -\sqrt{1 - x^2}$.

- Graph $y_1 = \sqrt{(1 - x^2)}$ and $y_2 = -\sqrt{(1 - x^2)}$ in several windows with different x-y dimension ratios. (We used parentheses around $1 - x^2$ because you will need them to enter the functions onto the Y= edit screen.) Continue until you obtain a graph that appears circular. *Note:* Gaps may appear near the x-axis.
- Graph $y_1 = \sqrt{1 - x^2}$ and $y_2 = -\sqrt{1 - x^2}$ in a square, friendly window.

Grapher Note: Some graphers have a ZSQUARE *feature that adjusts the window dimensions to make them match the physical proportions of the screen.*

Figure 1.11 shows three views. Only the view in part (a) looks circular because only in part (a) are the window dimensions proportional to the physical dimensions of the screen.

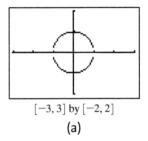

[−3, 3] by [−2, 2]

(a)

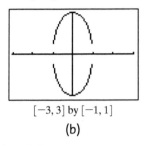

[−3, 3] by [−1, 1]

(b)

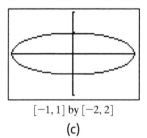

[−1, 1] by [−2, 2]

(c)

Figure 1.11 The graph of a circle in (a) a square window and (b and c) nonsquare windows.

Square, friendly, or standard windows are not always ideal. Example 4 illustrates that window dimensions may need to be exaggerated to reveal the important features of a graph.

Example 4 Finding Key Features of a Graph

Graph $f(x) = x^2(x + 7)^3$, using Xmin $= -10$ and Xmax $= 10$. Try various [Ymin, Ymax] settings.

Solution Figure 1.12 shows three possible views.

• Try the windows shown in Figure 1.12 and several others of your own choosing. Continue until you convince yourself that you have observed all the important features of $f(x) = x^2(x + 7)^3$ on the interval $[-10, 10]$.

Note that the view in part (c) shows more features of the graph than either part (a) or part (b) and hence is the best view of the three. Further investigation of the graph in other windows should reveal no other major features on the interval $[-10, 10]$.

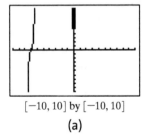

[−10, 10] by [−10, 10]

(a)

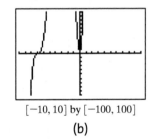

[−10, 10] by [−100, 100]

(b)

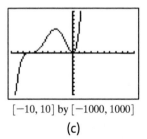

[−10, 10] by [−1000, 1000]

(c)

Figure 1.12 The graph of the same function in three different viewing windows.

Example 5 is designed to familiarize you with 12 basic graphs that are used in the textbook and are important as models in many fields of endeavor. You should learn these graphs by heart! That is, you should be able to sketch any of them quickly at any time without a great deal of thought, without doing any hand computation, and without using your grapher.

Example 5   Touring a Gallery of Basic Functions

Plot and explore the 12 graphs shown in Figure 1.13.

Solution   You may need to do some searching on your grapher keyboard or dig through some menus to find all these functions (CYGOM). You should use function notation—for example, abs (X) rather than abs X—even though your grapher may be forgiving.

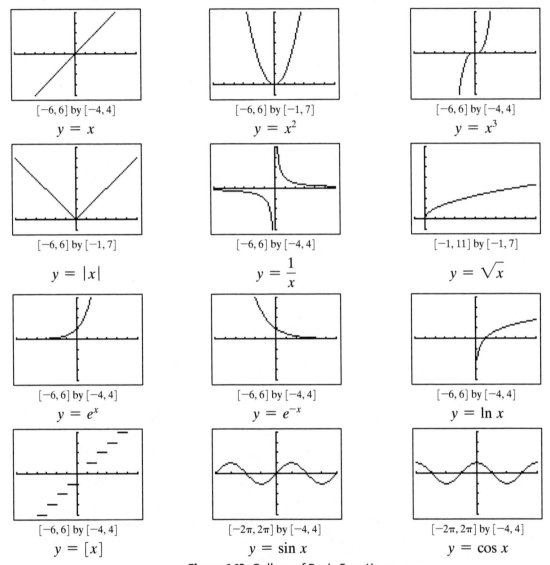

$$[-6, 6] \text{ by } [-4, 4]$$
$$y = x$$

$$[-6, 6] \text{ by } [-1, 7]$$
$$y = x^2$$

$$[-6, 6] \text{ by } [-4, 4]$$
$$y = x^3$$

$$[-6, 6] \text{ by } [-1, 7]$$
$$y = |x|$$

$$[-6, 6] \text{ by } [-4, 4]$$
$$y = \frac{1}{x}$$

$$[-1, 11] \text{ by } [-1, 7]$$
$$y = \sqrt{x}$$

$$[-6, 6] \text{ by } [-4, 4]$$
$$y = e^x$$

$$[-6, 6] \text{ by } [-4, 4]$$
$$y = e^{-x}$$

$$[-6, 6] \text{ by } [-4, 4]$$
$$y = \ln x$$

$$[-6, 6] \text{ by } [-4, 4]$$
$$y = [x]$$

$$[-2\pi, 2\pi] \text{ by } [-4, 4]$$
$$y = \sin x$$

$$[-2\pi, 2\pi] \text{ by } [-4, 4]$$
$$y = \cos x$$

Figure 1.13 Gallery of Basic Functions

- Graph all but the sine and cosine functions with the windows indicated in Figure 1.13. Regraph each function for other window dimensions, including standard, friendly, and square. Explore with TRACE.

- Graph the greatest integer function in CONNECTED mode and then in DOT mode. Which produces the better graph? Why?

- Graph the sine and cosine functions in DEGREE mode and then in RADIAN mode. Note that the graphs in Figure 1.13 are based on the use of RADIAN mode.

Grapher Note: *Some graphers have ZTRIG that automatically sets desirable window dimensions for viewing trigonometic functions.*

You should practice making hand-drawn sketches of the 12 basic functions until you can do them from memory.

1.5   Graphical Problem Solving

In this section we explore various grapher methods for solving equations and analyzing the graphical behavior of functions, so you should set your grapher to FUNCTION mode. We begin by showing how to solve equations graphically, using the example

$$|x| = x^2 + x - 2,$$

first by graphing

$$f(x) = |x| \quad \text{and} \quad g(x) = x^2 + x - 2$$

separately and then by investigating the related function

$$h(x) = f(x) - g(x) = |x| - (x^2 + x - 2).$$

Solving an Equation by Finding Intersections

We can solve an equation by graphing each side as a function and locating the points of intersection.

- Enter each side of the equation $|x| = x^2 + x - 2$ onto the Y= edit screen as shown in Figure 1.14.

- Graph the equations in a friendly window. See Figure 1.15.

Figure 1.14

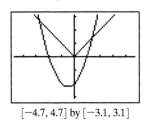

$[-4.7, 4.7]$ by $[-3.1, 3.1]$

Figure 1.15 The dimensions of a friendly window vary from grapher to grapher. Possible x dimensions are given in Table 1.2. ZDECIMAL or ZINTEGER yield a square, friendly window on some graphers.

The graph of f is V-shaped and the graph of g is an upward opening parabola. They have two points of intersection. Thus the equation $|x| = x^2 + x - 2$ has two solutions. These solutions are the x-coordinates (one positive and one negative) of the two points of intersection.

- Trace along either graph to approximate the positive solution, that is, to estimate the x-coordinate of the point of intersection in the first quadrant.

To get a better approximation for the positive solution we can *zoom in* by picking smaller and smaller windows that contain the point of intersection in the first quadrant. Three common ways to zoom in are to

1. change the WINDOW settings manually;

2. use ZOOMBOX, which lets you use the cursor to select the opposite corners of a "box" to define a new window; and

3. use ZOOMIN, which magnifies the graph around the cursor location by a factor that you can set.

- Practice each of the three types of zooming (CYGOM if necessary). Trace after each zoom step, as shown in Figure 1.16.

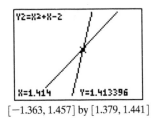

$[-1.363, 1.457]$ by $[1.379, 1.441]$

Figure 1.16 One possible view of the graphs after some zooming, with the TRACE feature activated.

Most graphers have an INTERSECTION feature that can be used to automate the process of solving equations graphically without adjusting the viewing window dimensions.

- Graph the equations of Figure 1.14 in a friendly window (Figure 1.15). Then use the INTERSECTION feature to locate the point of intersection in the first quadrant, as shown in Figure 1.17.

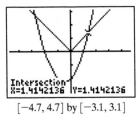

$[-4.7, 4.7]$ by $[-3.1, 3.1]$

Figure 1.17

Solving the equation $|x| = x^2 + x - 2$ algebraically reveals that the positive solution is $x = \sqrt{2} = 1.4142\ldots$, which confirms the graphical solution.

Solving by Finding x-Intercepts

To solve an equation of the form $f(x) = g(x)$, we can solve $f(x) - g(x) = 0$. Then the problem becomes one of finding where the functions $y = f - g$ and $y = 0$ intersect, or simply the x-intercepts of $y = f - g$. For example, to solve the equation $|x| = x^2 + x - 2$, we can find the x-intercepts of

$$y = h(x) = f(x) - g(x) = |x| - (x^2 + x - 2).$$

- Load the Y= edit screen, as shown in Figure 1.18a, selecting only $y_3 = y_1 - y_2 = \text{abs}(x) - (x^2 + x - 2)$ to be graphed.
- Graph y_3 in a friendly window, as shown in Figure 1.18b.
- The x-intercepts are also the "zeros" of the equation. Use the ZERO feature (CYGOM if necessary) to locate the negative x-intercept, as shown in Figure 1.18c.

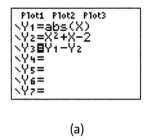

(a)

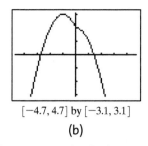

$[-4.7, 4.7]$ by $[-3.1, 3.1]$

(b)

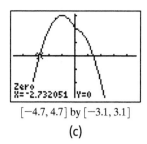

$[-4.7, 4.7]$ by $[-3.1, 3.1]$

(c)

Figure 1.18 Finding a solution of an equation by finding an *x*-intercept of the difference function.

Studying Graph Behavior

As you have seen, TRACE allows you to move from pixel to pixel on a graph with the coordinates of the points displayed to illustrate the numerical behavior of the function. For example, you can see whether the *y*-coordinate increases, decreases, or remains constant as *x* increases. ZOOMIN permits a "close-up" examination of the *local behavior* of graphs.

Three other grapher features are useful for investigating graph behavior (CYGOM if necessary).

1. VALUE evaluates a function for a given domain value, which often avoids the need for a friendly window.

2. MINIMUM finds a local minimum value of a function and the associated domain value.

3. MAXIMUM finds a local maximum value of a function and the associated domain value.

Example 6 Investigating Graph Behavior

Graph $f(x) = x^3 + 2x^2 - 5x - 6$ and study its behavior.

Solution Do the following on your grapher.

- Graph $y = f(x)$ in the standard window. Trace over until $x \approx -3.4$, as shown in Figure 1.19a. Then trace from left to right. Observe whether the function values (*y*-coordinates) increase, decrease, or remain constant as *x* increases.

- The graph appears to show that $f(2) = 0$, but TRACE fails to give a *y* value for $x = 2$. Use VALUE to find $f(2)$, as shown in Figure 1.19b.

- To determine precisely the intervals on which *f* is increasing or decreasing, locate the domain values at which the local maximums and minimums occur. Use MAXIMUM and MINIMUM to find these values. Figure 1.19c shows the result of using the MAXIMUM feature.

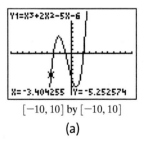

$[-10, 10]$ by $[-10, 10]$

(a)

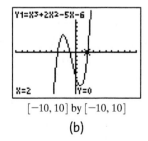

$[-10, 10]$ by $[-10, 10]$

(b)

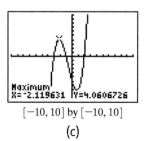

$[-10, 10]$ by $[-10, 10]$

(c)

Figure 1.19 Exploring a graph with (a) TRACE, (b) VALUE, and (c) MAXIMUM.

- Zoom in around the points that correspond to the local maximum and the local minimum. Describe the graph's behavior near each of these points.

What other behaviors of graphs can you study with the features of your grapher?

1.6 Parametric and Polar Graphing

Parametric Graphing

To graph parametric equations, set your grapher to PARAMETRIC mode. In PARAMETRIC mode, pressing [X,T,θ] will yield the independent variable t. The parametric equations

$$x(t) = \dots, \qquad y(t) = \dots$$

are entered in the form $x_1(t) = \dots, y_1(t) = \dots$ on the Y= edit screen.

Example 7 Graphing Parametric Equations

Graph the parametric equations.

$$x = t^2, \qquad y = t - 1 \qquad \text{for} \quad -2 \le t \le 2$$

Solution Follow these steps:

- Enter the parametric equations on the Y= edit screen, as shown in Figure 1.20.

Plot1 Plot2 Plot3
\X1T=T²
Y1T=T-1
\X2T=
Y2T=
\X3T=
Y3T=
\X4T=

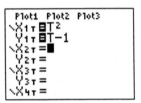

Figure 1.20

- Set the WINDOW dimensions shown in Figure 1.21. You will need to scroll down to see the entire menu given in Figure 1.21 because it has too many lines..

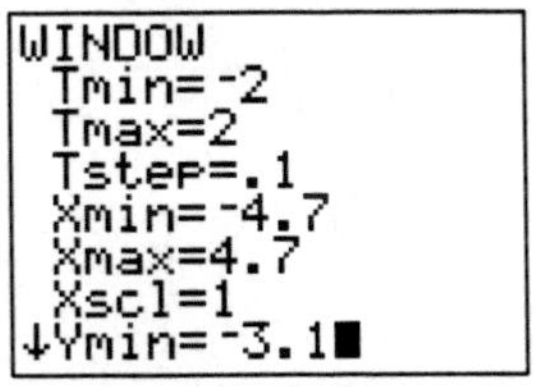

WINDOW
Tmin=-2
Tmax=2
Tstep=.1
Xmin=-4.7
Xmax=4.7
Xscl=1
↓Ymin=-3.1

Figure 1.21 Facsimile of the WINDOW screen set for plotting the parametric equations.

Tstep on the parametric WINDOW menu sets the step size between the successive t-values that the grapher uses to compute and plot (x, y) pairs. In this case, the Tstep of 0.1 will yield 40 steps from the Tmin of -2 to the Tmax of 2. Thus 41 points will be calculated and plotted, with the points corresponding to

$$t = -2.0, -1.9, -1.8, -1.7, \dots, 1.9, 2.0.$$

- Press [GRAPH] or [PLOT] to obtain the graph shown in Figure 1.22.

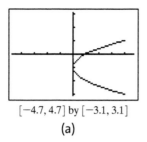

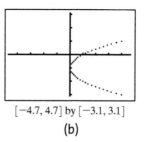

$[-4.7, 4.7]$ by $[-3.1, 3.1]$

(a)

$[-4.7, 4.7]$ by $[-3.1, 3.1]$

(b)

Figure 1.22 The graph in (a) CONNECTED mode and (b) DOT mode.

- Use TRACE to explore the graph numerically. Note that the values of the parameter t and the coordinates x and y are all shown on the screens in Figure 1.23.

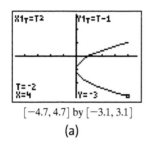

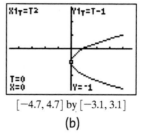

$[-4.7, 4.7]$ by $[-3.1, 3.1]$

(a)

$[-4.7, 4.7]$ by $[-3.1, 3.1]$

(b)

Figure 1.23 Two views of the parametric curve with TRACE activated.

Figures 1.22 and 1.23 show only a piece of the parabola $x = (y + 1)^2$ rather than the complete parabola for this viewing window. The parametric WINDOW menu allows you to choose a part of the graph by setting Tmin and Tmax. Do you see why? If not, experiment with the Tmin and Tmax settings until you do.

Polar Graphing

To graph polar equations set your grapher to POLAR mode. Pressing $\boxed{\text{X,T,}\theta}$ will yield the independent variable θ.

Example 8 Graphing Polar Equations

Simultaneously graph *r = 9 sin 5θ and r = 9*.

Solution Follow these steps:

- Set your grapher to SIMULTANEOUS and RADIAN modes. Then enter the polar equations on the Y= edit screen, as shown in Figure 1.24.

Figure 1.24

- Set the WINDOW dimensions to

$$\theta\text{min} = 0, \qquad \theta\text{max} = 2\pi, \qquad \theta\text{step} = \pi/24,$$

using the standard dimension of $[-10, 10]$ by $[-10, 10]$ for x and y. (On some graphers, you can obtain these settings by using ZSTANDARD.)

- Press GRAPH or PLOT to obtain the graphs shown in Figure 1.25.

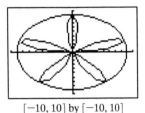

[−10, 10] by [−10, 10]

Figure 1.25 The circle $r = 9$ and the 5-petaled rose $r = 9 \sin 5\theta$.

- Trace along the two polar curves.
- Set θ max $= \pi$. Then use ZSQUARE to square the viewing window. If no such command is available on your grapher, reset the x-dimensions of the WINDOW menu by hand. Figure 1.26 shows the result.

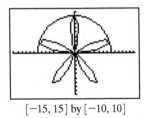

[−15, 15] by [−10, 10]

Figure 1.26

Note that the entire rose curve is plotted for the interval $0 \le \theta \le \pi$. Explore the effect of changing the 5 in the equation $r = 9 \sin 5\theta$ to another number.

1.7   Curve Fitting and Statistics

A grapher can help you organize, process, and analyze data, as well as compute and plot models for paired data. The procedures for data analysis and curve fitting vary a great deal from grapher to grapher (CYGOM for details).

Example 9 Plotting and Fitting Data

Plot the national debt data given in Table 1.3, find a model for the data, and then overlay a graph of the model on the scatter plot.

Table 1.3 U.S. Public Debt, 1950–1990

Year	Debt (Billions of dollars)
1950	256.1
1960	284.1
1970	370.1
1975	533.2
1980	907.7
1985	1,823.1
1990	3,233.3

Source: The World Almanac and Book of Facts (1995, Mahwah, N.J.: Funk & Wagnalls), p. 109.

Solution Follow these steps:

- Enter the data shown in Table 1.3 into the statistical memory of your grapher, as shown in Figure 1.27a.

- Set an appropriate window for the data, letting x be the year and y be the amount of the debt, as shown in Figure 1.27b.

- Make a scatter plot of the data, as shown in Figure 1.27c.

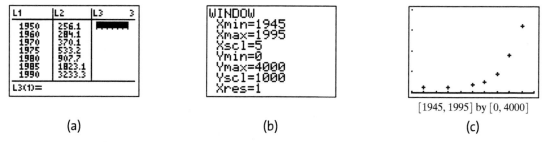

[1945, 1995] by [0, 4000]

(a)   (b)   (c)

Figure 1.27 The steps involved in making a scatter plot on a grapher.

Most graphers have several regression options. Typically, linear, quadratic, exponential, logarithmic, and power functions are available as regression models. Some graphers offer other options. The following activity illustrates quadratic regression. That is, we find a quadratic function that closely fits the given data.

- Choose the QUADRATIC option from your grapher's regression menu. Use the first column of data for the x-values and the second column as y-values. The grapher should return approximate coefficients for the quadratic regression equation, as shown in Figure 1.28a.

- Load the regression equation onto the Y= edit screen, as shown in Fiugre 1.28b.

- Press $\boxed{\text{GRAPH}}$ or $\boxed{\text{PLOT}}$ to obtain the graph in Figure 1.28c, which shows both the scatter plot and the graph of the regression equation.

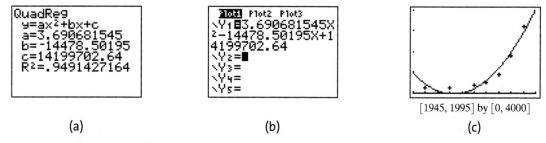

[1945, 1995] by [0, 4000]

(a)   (b)   (c)

Figure 1.28 The steps involved in fitting a quadratic function to a scatter plot.

Repeat the steps to find and graph other regression equations for the data.

Most graphers offer a variety of statistical plots, often including histograms, boxplots, and line graphs. In addition, graphers can carry out many types of statistical computations (CYGOM for details).

1.8 Matrix Calculations

A grapher can perform many matrix operations, thus avoiding the tedium of hand computation. Matrix procedures vary somewhat from grapher to grapher (CYGOM for details).

- Place matrix *A* on the Home screen (Figure 1.29a) and compute its determinant (Figure 1.29b).

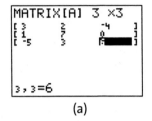

(a)

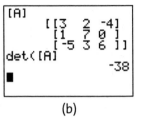

(b)

Figure 1.29 (a) Matrix entry and (b) matrix display and determinant calculation.

- Compute the inverse of matrix *A*. You may need to scroll, using ▶ in order to see the entire answer (Figure 1.30).

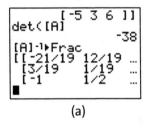

(a)

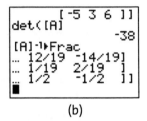

(b)

Figure 1.30 (a) Computing the inverse of matrix *A* and (b) scrolling.

***Grapher Note:** In Figure 1.30a, we used the* FRAC *feature to convert the decimal entries of A^{-1} to fractions.*

- Enter the matrix $B = \begin{pmatrix} 12 \\ 9 \\ -13 \end{pmatrix}$ into the matrix editor of your grapher (Figure 1.31a).

- Compute the product $A^{-1} \cdot B$ on the Home screen (Figure 1.31b).

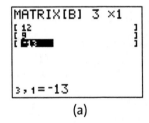

(a)

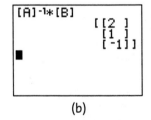

(b)

Figure 1.31 (a) Entering a column matrix and (b) multiplying matrices.

Graphers have other matrix features. Most importantly, many graphers can perform elementary row operations on a matrix.

1.9   Grapher Insights and Caveats

Limitations of Grapher Computations

Grapher computations are limited in *magnitude* and *relative accuracy*. Numbers less than the lower magnitude limit are rounded to zero. Numbers greater than or equal to the upper magnitude limit yield *overflow errors.*

Regarding relative error, some graphers store only the first 13 significant digits of a number (the rest of the number is rounded off) and they display at most 10 digits. To see this in action,

- Enter $(2/3 - 1/3) - 1/3$ on your grapher.

We know that $(2/3 - 1/3) - 1/3 = 0$, but older graphers will not give 0 as the final result. What steps in the grapher computation could have produced this result? Explain.

How a Grapher Draws a Function Graph

All graphers produce graphs, or plots, by lighting pixels on a liquid crystal display (LCD). Figure 1.33a shows the graph of a line on an LCD, and Figure 1.33b shows how it might appear under a magnifying glass. When the grapher is in CONNECTED mode, the plotted pixels are connected by "line segments" of pixels. When in DOT mode, the pixels are left unconnected.

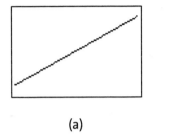

(a)

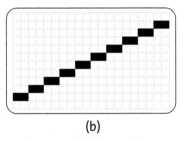

(b)

Figure 1.33 (a) The graph of a line on an LCD and (b) how it looks under magnification.

Limitations of Grapher Plotting

Grapher plotting is limited by roundoff error in the calculation of the y-coordinates from the function formula. More significantly, grapher plotting is limited because, for each point plotted, a pixel is rarely centered on the LCD at the exact vertical location corresponding to the y-coordinate of the point.

Despite these limitations, graphers can quickly produce accurate graphs for most functions described in this book if the viewing dimensions are chosen appropriately. It takes mathematical and grapher experience to get good at choosing windows. You will develop this skill over time as you go through the workshop exercises and the rest of the book.

Interpreting Grapher Plots

As Examples 3 and 4 illustrated, a grapher plot may be misleading or incomplete. (See Figures 1.11 and 1.12.) True visualization occurs in the "mind's eye" when you use the information gained from a grapher together with your mathematical knowledge to obtain a mental image of the mathematical graph. To communicate this mental visualization to another person, however, you must learn to describe and draw graphs accurately. When recording a graph on paper, you should normally add suggestive arrowheads and label axes, key points, and other pertinent information. Figure 1.34 shows how two rather misleading views of a complicated graph can be combined into a single recorded graph. This is a skill to strive for as you work with the grapher.

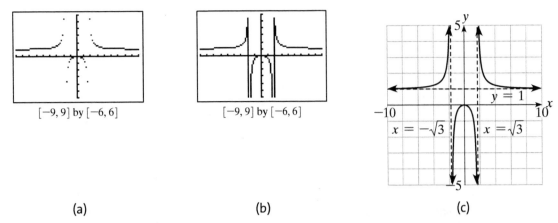

$[-9, 9]$ by $[-6, 6]$ $[-9, 9]$ by $[-6, 6]$

(a)   (b)   (c)

Figure 1.34 The graph of $y = x^2/(x^2 - 3)$ as shown (a and b) on a grapher and (c) on paper.

1.10   Viewing Window Summary

Choosing a Viewing Window

You need experience and mathematical expectations to choose appropriate viewing windows. One approach is to start with the *standard window* of $[-10, 10]$ by $[-10, 10]$ and adjust the y-dimensions.

Some windows may show more features of a graph than others. The view on the right shows the key features of the graph; the other two views do not.

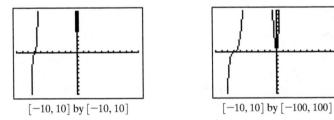

$[-10, 10]$ by $[-10, 10]$ $[-10, 10]$ by $[-100, 100]$ $[-10, 10]$ by $[-1000, 1000]$

Figure 1.35 Three views of $f(x) = x^2(x + 7)^3$.

Friendly Windows

Your choice of Xmin and Xmax affect the x-coordinate readout when you *trace* along a graph. You can use the [Xmin, Xmax] settings given in the table, or positive integer multiples of these settings, to guarantee a *friendly* x-coordinate readout when tracing. Windows with friendly x-coordinates are called *friendly windows*.

Table 1.4 The [Xmin, Xmax] dimensions for a basic friendly window on various graphers.

Grapher	[Xmin, Xmax]
TI-80	[–3.1, 3.1]
Casio, Sharp, TI-82, TI-83	[–4.7, 4.7]
TI-81	[–4.8, 4.7]
TI-85	[–6.3, 6.3]
Hewlett-Packard	[–6.5, 6.5]
TI-92	[–11.9, 11.9]

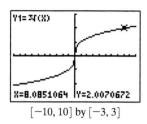

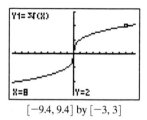

$[-10, 10]$ by $[-3, 3]$

$[-9.4, 9.4]$ by $[-3, 3]$

Figure 1.36 Graphs of $f(x) = \sqrt[3]{x}$

Square Windows

A *square window* is a window that shows the true shape of a graph. Such a window makes perpendicular lines look perpendicular, a square look square, and a circle look circular. A square window has the same proportions as your grapher screen. Many grapher screens have a width-to-height ratio of $3 : 2$. Most graphers have a built-in feature for squaring windows.

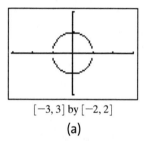

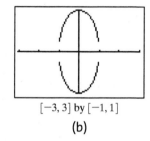

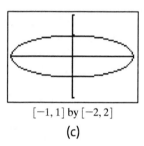

$[-3, 3]$ by $[-2, 2]$

(a)

$[-3, 3]$ by $[-1, 1]$

(b)

$[-1, 1]$ by $[-2, 2]$

(c)

Figure 1.37 Three views of the circle $x^2 + y^2 = 1$.

Integer and Decimal Windows

These windows are special types of friendly windows. An *integer window* is a window in which each pixel is centered at a point with integer coordintes and the change in both x and y is 1. A *decimal window* is a window in which each pixel is centered at a point with coordinates of at most one decimal place and the change in both x and y is 0.1. On most graphers, both integer and decimal windows are square and friendly.

1.11   Exercises for Chapter 1

The exercises are correlated with the sections of the Grapher Workshop. If any give you difficulty, resolve it by consulting either your owner's manual or your instructor.

Numerical Computation and Editing

In Exercises 1–6, use a grapher to evaluate the expression.

1. 600×1.075^2

2. 1.3^5

3. $\log(1/10)$

4. $|-7|$

5. $\sqrt[3]{64}$

6. $\sqrt[4]{81}$

In Exercises 7 and 8, use ANS.

7. Calculate the first seven terms in the geometric sequence that begins with 2 and grows by a constant factor of 6: 2, 12, 72, ...

8. Calculate the first seven terms in the arithmetic sequence that begins with 4 and grows by a constant 9: 4, 13, 22, ...

In Exercises 9 and 10, use replay.

9. Evaluate $f(x) = x^2 + x - 2$ at $x = -3, -2.5, 3$.

10. Evaluate $g(t) = 2t^3 - |5t|$ at $t = -2, 3.4, 7$.

Table Building

In Exercises 11–14, make a table with the following inputs.

  a. $x = -3, -2, -1, \ldots, 3$

  b. $x = 0, 1, 2, \ldots, 6$

  c. $x = -10, -5, 0, \ldots, 20$

11. $f(x) = x^2 + 15$

12. $f(x) = \ln(x^2 + 1)$

13. $f(x) = |x - 2|$

14. $f(x) = \sqrt[3]{x^2 + x - 2}$

Function Graphing

In Exercises 15–20, graph the function in each type of window.

  a. The standard window

  b. A square window containing the standard window

  c. A friendly window using TRACE to support the friendly x-coordinate readout

  d. A window that is both square and friendly

15. $y = 3x - 2$

16. $y = -\frac{1}{2}x + 3$

17. $y = 1 - x^2$

18. $y = 2x^2 - 3x + 1$

19. $y = |x + 2|$

20. $y = \sqrt{9 - x^2}$

In Exercises 21 and 22, explain any differences in the two modes.

21. Enter and graph

  $y_1 = 2x + 1;$

  $y_2 = 2x + 2;$

  $y_3 = 2x + 3.$

  Switch between SEQUENTIAL and SIMULTANEOUS modes and draw the graphs again.

22. Graph $y = 3x - 1$. Switch between CONNECTED and DOT modes and draw the graph again.

In Exercises 23 and 24, find a window that reveals the key features of the function. How many x-intercepts does the graph have?

23. $y = x^2(x - 12)$

24. $y = x(x + 3)^2(x + 14)$

Graphical Problem Solving

In Exercises 25–28, solve the equation by
   a. finding intersections.
   b. finding x-intercepts.

25. $|x| = \frac{1}{2}x + 1$

26. $|x - 3| = -\frac{1}{2}x + 4$

27. $x - 2 = 1 - x^2$

28. $x - 3 = x^2 - 5$

In Exercises 29 and 30, (a) find a viewing window that reveals the key features of the graph, and (b) find the local maximum and minimum values.

29. $y = x^2(x - 12)$

30. $y = x(x + 3)^2(x + 14)$

Parametric and Polar Graphing

In Exercises 31–34, use PARAMETRIC mode.

31. Enter

$$x(t) = t, \qquad y(t) = t.$$

Predict what will happen as a result of the WINDOW settings for t. Then graph and compare with your prediction.

   a. Tmin $= -10$, Tmax $= 10$, Tstep $= 0.1$

   b. Tmin $= 0$, Tmax $= 10$, Tstep $= 0.1$

   c. Tmin $= -10$, Tmax $= 0$, Tstep $= 0.1$

   d. Tmin $= -10$, Tmax $= 10$, Tstep $= 1$

   e. Tmin $= -5$, Tmax $= 5$, Tstep $= 1$

   f. Tmin $= 10$, Tmax $= -10$, Tstep $= -0.1$

32. Graph

$$x_1(t) = t, \qquad y_1(t) = 2t;$$
$$x_2(t) = 2t, \qquad y_2(t) = t,$$

with Tmin $= -10$, Tmax $= 10$, Tstep $= 0.1$. Predict what the graphs will look like. Then graph and compare with your prediction.

33. Graph

$$x_1(t) = 2t, \qquad y_1(t) = t^2,$$

with Tmin $= -10$, Tmax $= 10$, Tstep $= 0.1$.

34. Graph
$$x_1(t) = 2t, \qquad y_1(t) = t^2;$$
$$x_2(t) = y_1(t), \quad y_2(t) = x_1(t),$$
with Tmin $= -10$, Tmax $= 10$, Tstep $= 0.1$.

In Exercises 35–38, use POLAR and RADIAN modes.

35. Graph $r = 6$ in a square window. Switch between CONNECTED and DOT modes and graph again.

36. Graph $r = 2\cos\theta$ in a square window. Switch between CONNECTED and DOT modes and graph again.

37. Graph $r_1 = 2$ and $r_2 = 5$. Switch between SEQUENTIAL and SIMULTANEOUS modes and graph again.

38. Graph $r_1 = 2$ and $r_2 = 2\cos 3\theta$. Switch beween SEQUENTIAL and SIMULTANEOUS modes and graph again.

Curve Fitting and Statistics

In Exercises 39 and 40, use the data in Table 1.5.

Table 1.5 Official Census Population (in millions of persons), 1900–1990

Year	Florida	Pennsylvania
1900	0.5	6.3
1910	0.8	7.7
1920	1.0	8.7
1930	1.5	9.6
1940	1.9	9.9
1950	2.7	10.5
1960	5.0	11.3
1970	6.8	11.8
1980	9.7	11.9
1990	12.9	11.9

Source: U.S. Census Bureau as reported in *The World Almanac and Book of Facts* (1995, Mahwah, N.J.: Funk & Wagnalls), p. 377.

39. a. Enter the Florida population data into the statistical memory of your grapher.

   b. Set an appropriate window for the data and make a scatter plot.

   c. Choose the EXPONENTIAL option from your grapher's regression menu to find the constants in the regression equation.

   d. Load the regression equation onto the Y = edit screen and overlay the graph of the regression equation on the scatter plot.

40. a. Enter the Pennsylvania population data into the statistical memory of your grapher.

   b. Set an appropriate window for the data and make a scatter plot.

   c. Choose the LINEAR option from your grapher's regression menu to find the coefficients for the linear regression equation.

    d. Load the regression equation onto the Y $=$ edit screen and overlay the graph of the regression equation on the scatter plot.

Matrix Calculations

In Exercises 41 and 42, perform the computations.

41. a. Enter the matrix

$$A = \begin{pmatrix} 1 & -3 \\ 5 & 2 \end{pmatrix}$$

      into the matrix editor of your grapher and compute its determinant.

    b. Compute the inverse of matrix A.

    c. Enter the matrix

$$B = \begin{pmatrix} -1 \\ 12 \end{pmatrix}$$

      into the matrix editor of your grapher and compute the product $A^{-1} \cdot B$.

42. a. Enter the matrix

$$A = \begin{pmatrix} 4 & 2 & -1 \\ 1 & -1 & 0 \\ 0 & 3 & 5 \end{pmatrix}$$

      into the matrix editor of your grapher and compute its determinant.

    b. Compute the inverse of matrix A.

    c. Enter the matrix

$$B = \begin{pmatrix} 15 \\ 2 \\ -2 \end{pmatrix}$$

      into the matrix editor of your grapher and compute the product $A^{-1} \cdot B$.

Grapher Insights and Caveats

In Exercises 43 and 44, sketch the graph.

43. Graph

$$y = \frac{(x + 3)^2}{x(x + 4)}$$

    in CONNECTED and DOT modes and then sketch the graph on paper.

44. Graph

$$y = \frac{x(x - 3)}{(x - 1)(x + 4)}$$

    in CONNECTED and DOT modes and then sketch the graph on paper.

2

TI-82, TI-83, and TI-83 Plus Graphing Calculators

These three graphing calculators are versatile tools for exploring mathematics. In addition to all of the features of a scientific calculator, they have large-screen computation and programming capabilities and built-in software for working with graphs, tables, lists, matrices, sequences, probability, and statistics. Hence, these calculators are actually powerful, user-friendly hand-held computers.

This chapter is designed to familiarize you with many aspects of these calculators. The three models are so similar that in most cases you can follow the same instructions, and we will refer to "your calculator," rather than the particular model number. When they do differ, specific instructions will be given for the TI-82, TI-83, and the TI-83 Plus. Also, unless otherwise noted, both the TI-83 and TI-83 Plus will be referred to as the TI-83.

Have the calculator out and "on" so that you can work through the examples as you read this chapter. Feel free to explore the menus and features of your calculator. A few hours of productive play can help you reach a comfort level so that you can readily solve problems using this powerful tool.

2.1 Getting Started

2.1.1 Exploring the Keyboard

Take a minute to study the keys on your calculator. There are 10 rows of keys, each with five keys, except for the four specially arranged cursor-movement keys. These keys are divided into three zones.

- **Row 1**
  Used for graphing and table building.

- **Rows 2, 3, and 4**
  Used for accessing menus and editing.

- **Rows 5–10**
  Used like those on a scientific calculator.

Thinking in terms of these three zones will help you find keys on your calculator.

2.1.2 Using the Multipurpose ON Key

The On key ON is in the lower left-hand corner of the keyboard. It is used to do the following:

- Turn on the calculator.

- Interrupt graphing if you want to stop before a graph is completely drawn.

- Interrupt program execution to break out of a program.

- Turn off the calculator. To do this, press

$$\boxed{\text{2nd}} \quad \boxed{\text{ON}}.$$

Note that the word OFF is written in colored letters just above $\boxed{\text{ON}}$ and that the color of the letters matches that of $\boxed{\text{2nd}}$. In the future, we say, "press $\boxed{\text{2nd}}$ $\boxed{\text{OFF}}$."

To prolong the life of the batteries, your calculator automatically turns itself off after several minutes have elapsed without any activity. To turn on your calculator in these circumstances, press

$$\boxed{\text{ON}}.$$

Your calculator will turn on and return you to the screen on which you were working when it turned itself off.

2.1.3 Adjusting the Screen Contrast

You can adjust the screen contrast as needed, choosing from 10 contrast settings that range from 0 (the lightest) to 9 (the darkest).

To darken the screen,
1. press and release $\boxed{\text{2nd}}$ and then
2. press and hold $\boxed{\blacktriangle}$.

To lighten the screen,
1. press and release $\boxed{\text{2nd}}$ and then
2. press and hold $\boxed{\blacktriangledown}$.

If you find it necessary to set the contrast at 8 or 9, it is probably time to change your batteries. (Your calculator uses four AAA batteries.) If after you change the batteries the screen is too dark, simply adjust contrast following the steps outlined above.

2.2 Calculating and Editing

2.2.1 Returning to the Home Screen

Computation is done on the Home screen. To help you remember how to get to the Home screen from other screens and menus, remember the sentence, "Quit to go Home." This means that if you get lost in a menu and want to return to the Home screen, press

$$\boxed{\text{2nd}} \quad \boxed{\text{QUIT}}.$$

($\boxed{\text{QUIT}}$ is the second function of $\boxed{\text{MODE}}$ located to the right of $\boxed{\text{2nd}}$.) If your calculator does not respond to this command, it is probably busy graphing or running a program. In this case, press

$$\boxed{\text{ON}} \text{ and then } \boxed{\text{2nd}} \quad \boxed{\text{QUIT}}.$$

2.2.2 Performing Simple Calculations

1. To compute $2 + 5 \times 8$, press:

$$2 \boxed{+} 5 \boxed{\times} 8 \boxed{\text{ENTER}}.$$

Your screen should look like Figure 2.1.

2. Find the value of log(100) by pressing
   - on the TI-82 $\boxed{\text{LOG}}$ $\boxed{(}$ **100** $\boxed{)}$ $\boxed{\text{ENTER}}$, or
   - on the TI-83 $\boxed{\text{LOG}}$ **100** $\boxed{)}$ $\boxed{\text{ENTER}}$.

Note that on the TI-83 the left parenthesis automatically appears after pressing $\boxed{\text{LOG}}$. Your screen should look like Figure 2.2.

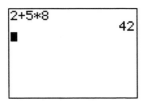

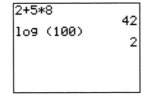

| Figure 2.1 | Figure 2.2 |

Note: Do not type the letters L, O, and G. The calculator would interpret this as implied multiplication of the variables L, O, and G.

2.2.3 Working with Error Messages

Your calculator knows the difference between the binary operation of subtraction (the blue ⎡ − ⎤) and the additive inverse, or "sign change," operation (the gray or white ⎡ (−) ⎤). To learn how the calculator handles errors related to these keys, let's purposely make a mistake. Enter the following key sequence:

$$7 \boxed{+} \boxed{-} 4 \text{ ENTER}.$$

Your calculator should respond as shown in Figure 2.3. In this case the *error message* indicates you have made a syntax error and have two choices. This ERROR MESSAGE menu is typical of all numbered menus on your calculator. To select an item from a numbered menu, do either of the following:

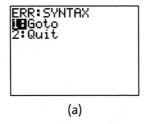

(a)

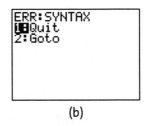

(b)

Figure 2.3 The ERROR MESSAGE menu on the (a) TI-82 and (b) TI-83.

a. press the number to the left of the choice you want—this is the fastest way—or

b. position the cursor next to your choice and press ENTER.

To return to the Home screen (Remember, "Quit to go Home."), press

⎡ 2nd ⎤ ⎡QUIT⎤,

or press the number that corresponds to ⎡QUIT⎤ on your calculator. Choose Quit.

The screen should look like Figure 2.4, with a flashing cursor below the 7.

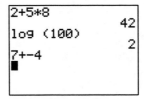

Figure 2.4

To return to the ERROR MESSAGE menu (see Fig. 2.3), press

ENTER.

Selecting the Goto option at this point causes the cursor to go to the source of the error and clears the Home screen of all data except the expression that contains the error. Generally, the Goto option will help you find your error.

1. If you have not already done so, choose the Goto option now.

The cursor should flash on the subtraction symbol.

2. Press $\boxed{(-)}$ to overwrite the subtraction symbol with a negative sign.

3. Press $\boxed{\text{ENTER}}$ to re-execute the calculation.

You should obtain the expected result: 3.

2.2.4   Editing Expressions

Using Last Entry.   When you press $\boxed{\text{ENTER}}$ on the Home screen to evaluate an expression or execute an instruction, the expression or instruction is stored with other previous entries in a storage area called the Last Entry Stack. You can recall a prior entry from the Last Entry Stack, edit it, and then execute the edited instruction, as the following example illustrates.

Example 1   Doubling an Investment's Value

Problem   You deposit $500 in a savings account with a 4.75% annual percentage rate (APR), compounded monthly. How long will it take for your investment to double in value?

Solution   Because $4.75 \approx 5$ and $100 \div 5 = 20$, you might make an initial guess of 20 years. To check the guess, do the following:

1. Press $\boxed{\text{2nd}}$ $\boxed{\text{QUIT}}$ to return to the Home screen, if necessary.

2. Press $\boxed{\text{CLEAR}}$ once or twice.

   On a line with text on the Home screen, $\boxed{\text{CLEAR}}$ clears the text from the line.

   On a blank line on the Home screen, $\boxed{\text{CLEAR}}$ clears the text from the entire screen.

3. Press **500** $\boxed{(}$ **1** $\boxed{+}$ **0.0475** $\boxed{\div}$ **12** $\boxed{)}$ $\boxed{\wedge}$ $\boxed{(}$ **12** $\boxed{\times}$ **20** $\boxed{)}$ $\boxed{\text{ENTER}}$.
   (See Fig. 2.5.)

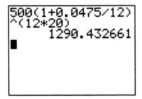

Figure 2.5

4. To display the results in a format more appropriate for calculations involving money,

   a. Press $\boxed{\text{MODE}}$ to display the MODE screen.

   b. Press $\boxed{\blacktriangledown}$ $\boxed{\blacktriangleright}$ $\boxed{\blacktriangleright}$ $\boxed{\blacktriangleright}$ to position the cursor over the 2.

   c. Press $\boxed{\text{ENTER}}$.

The numerical display format is changed to two fixed decimal places (see Fig. 2.6).

(a)   (b)

Figure 2.6 The Mode screen on the (a) TI-82 and (b) TI-83.

5. Press $\boxed{\text{2nd}}$ $\boxed{\text{QUIT}}$ to return to the Home screen.

6. Press $\boxed{\text{ENTER}}$ to display the result in the two-decimal-place format (see Fig. 2.7).

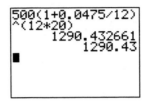

Figure 2.7

Our next guess should be quite a bit less than 20 years, say 14 years. In this case, do the following:

1. To edit the old expression, press $\boxed{\text{2nd}}$ $\boxed{\text{ENTRY}}$ $\boxed{\blacktriangleleft}$ $\boxed{\blacktriangleleft}$ $\boxed{\blacktriangleleft}$ **14.**

2. Evaluate the edited version by pressing $\boxed{\text{ENTER}}$ (see Fig. 2.8).

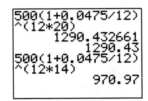

Figure 2.8

3. To change the number of years to 14.5, press

$\boxed{\text{2nd}}$ $\boxed{\text{ENTRY}}$ $\boxed{\blacktriangleleft}$ $\boxed{\text{.}}$ 5 $\boxed{\text{ENTER}}$.

Notice that the final parenthesis can be left off and that all three results can be seen on the screen (see Fig. 2.9).

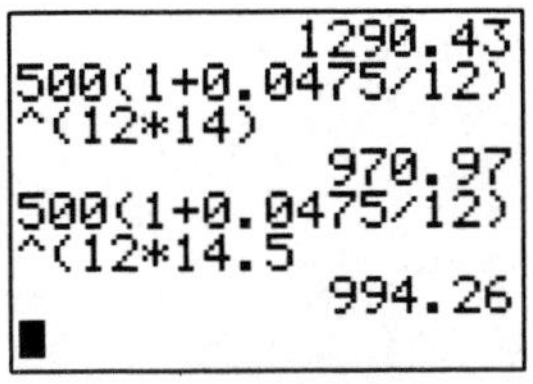

Figure 2.9

Continue this guess-and-check procedure until you obtain the accuracy you desire. Press $\boxed{\text{2nd}}$ $\boxed{\text{ENTRY}}$ several times to observe how the Last Entry Stack has stored several prior entries.

Display Cursors.   There are four types of display cursors. Each of these cursors indicates what will happen when you press the next key (see Table 2.1).

Table 2.1 Display cursors.

Entry cursor	Solid blinking rectangle	The next keystroke is entered at the cursor; it overwrites any character.
INS (insert) cursor	Blinking underline	The next keystroke is inserted in front of the cursor location.
2nd cursor	Blinking ↑	The next keystroke is a 2nd operation.
ALPHA cursor	Blinking A	The next keystroke is an alphabetic character. The SOLVE command may be executed on the TI-83.

Using the Edit Keys.   The Edit keys help you make effective use of your calculator. Study Table 2.2.

Table 2.2 Edit keys.

Key	Comments
◄ or ►	Moves the cursor within a line. These keys repeat.
▲ or ▼	Moves the cursor between the lines. These keys repeat.
2nd ◄	Moves the cursor to the beginning of the expression. Can be used for fast-tracing on the Graph screen.
2nd ►	Moves the cursor to the end of the expression. Can be used for fast-tracing on the Graph screen.
ENTER	Evaluates an expression or executes an instruction. This key acts as a Pause key when graphing, press it a second time to resume graphing.
CLEAR	• On a line with text on the Home screen, this key clears (blanks) the current command line. • On a blank line on the Home screen, it clears the screen. • In an editor, it clears (blanks) the expression or value on which the cursor is located. It does not store zero as the value.
DEL	Deletes the character at the cursor. This key repeats.
2nd |INS|	Inserts characters at the underline cursor. To end the insertion, press 2nd |INS| or a cursor-movement key.
2nd	Means the next key pressed is a 2nd operation (the color-coded operation to the left above a key). The cursor changes to an ↑. To cancel 2nd, press 2nd again.
ALPHA	Means the next key pressed is an ALPHA character (the color-coded character to the right above a key). The cursor changes to an A. To cancel ALPHA, press ALPHA or a cursor-movement key.
2nd |A-LOCK|	Sets ALPHA-LOCK. Each subsequent key press is an ALPHA character. The cursor changes to an A. To cancel ALPHA-LOCK, press ALPHA Note that prompts for names automatically set the keyboard in ALPHA-LOCK.
X,T,θ	Allows you to enter an X in Function (Func) mode, a T in Parametric (Par) mode, or a θ in Polar (Pol) mode without pressing ALPHA first. Additionally on the TI-83, the key X,T,θ,n allows you to enter an n in Sequence (Seq) mode.

2.2.5 Scientific Notation and the Answer Key

Example 2 illustrates a geometric progression—a sequence of numbers that grows by a constant factor—while demonstrating some important features of your calculator.

Example 2 Generating a Geometric Sequence

Problem Display the first few terms of the sequence that begins with 1.7×10^3 and grows by a factor of 100.

Solution To generate the sequence, do the following:

1. Return your calculator to Floating Point Numerical Display (Float) mode by pressing
    MODE ▼ ENTER .

2. Press [2nd] [QUIT] to return to the Home screen.

3. Clear the Home screen by pressing [CLEAR] [CLEAR].

4. To enter 1.7×10^3 onto the Home screen, press **1.7** [2nd] [EE] **3** [ENTER].

Notice that entering the number in scientific notation did not cause the result to be displayed in scientific notation (see Fig. 2.10).

5. Press [×] **100.**

As soon as you press [×], 'Ans *' is displayed on the screen. **Ans** is a variable that contains the last calculated result (see Fig. 2.11).

Figure 2.10

Figure 2.11

6. Press [ENTER] four times.

Each time you press [ENTER], the previous answer is multiplied by 100 and Ans is updated. Notice that the displayed values automatically change to scientific notation after the third iteration (see Fig. 2.12).

7. Press [ENTER] twice to see the geometric progression continue (see Fig. 2.13).

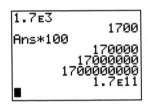

Figure 2.12

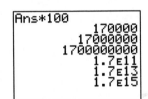

Figure 2.13

2.2.6   Other Computation Features and Menus

Clear the Home screen and then try the following calculations.

1. **Integer Arithmetic**

   To calculate $-2 - (-3) + (-4) \times 5$, press

   $\qquad$ [(−)] **2** [−] [(−)] **3** [+] [(−)] **4** [×] **5** [ENTER].

2. **Rational-number arithmetic**

   To add the fractions $\frac{1}{3}$ and $\frac{4}{7}$, press

   $\qquad$ **1** [÷] **3** [+] **4** [÷] **7** [MATH] [1: Frac] [ENTER].

3. **Real-number arithmetic**

   To approximate the principal square root of 10, press

   - on the TI-82 [2nd] [√‾] [( ] **10** [ )] [ENTER].

   - on the TI-83 [2nd] [√‾] **10** [ )] [ENTER].

   (See Fig. 2.14.)

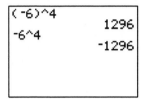

```
-2--3+ -4*5
             -19
1/3+4/7▶Frac
           19/21
√(10)
        3.16227766
```

Figure 2.14

4. **Order of operations**

   To show that exponents take precedence over negation, and thus $(-6)^4 \neq -6^4$, press

   CLEAR ((−) **6**) ^ **4** ENTER.

   Then press

   (−) **6** ^ **4** ENTER.

   and compare the results (see Fig. 2.15).

```
(-6)^4
            1296
-6^4
           -1296
```

Figure 2.15

5. **Trig and angle computation**

   To calculate tan 60° without switching to Degree mode, press

   CLEAR TAN **60** 2nd |ANGLE| [1: °] ENTER.

   Then press

   2nd |√⁻| 3 ENTER.

   and compare the results. Re-enter these expressions adding parentheses as needed to match Figure 2.16

6. **Roots**

   To evaluate $\sqrt[5]{-16807}$, press either

   CLEAR **5** MATH [5 : √] (−) **16807** ENTER.

   or

   $\overset{x}{}$

   ((−) **16807**) ^ (**1** ÷ **5**) ENTER.

   (See Fig. 2.17).

7. **Greatest integer function**

   To determine the greatest integer less than or equal to −4.916, press

   - on the TI-82 MATH ▶ [4 : int] (−) **4.916** ENTER, or
   - on the TI-83 MATH ▶ [5 : int] (−) **4.916** ENTER.

   Add parentheses if you wish to match Figure 2.18.

8. **Factorial**

   To evaluate $10! = 10 \cdot 9 \cdot 8 \cdot 7 \cdot 6 \cdot 5 \cdot 4 \cdot 3 \cdot 2 \cdot 1$, press

   10 MATH ◀ [4 : !] ENTER.

   (See Fig. 2.18)

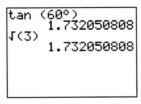

Figure 2.16

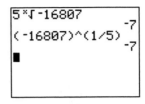

Figure 2.17

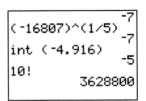

Figure 2.18

2.2.7   Computing with Lists

Set the display format to five fixed decimal places as follows:

1. Press MODE.
2. Press ▼ and then ► six times.
3. Press ENTER.
4. Return to the Home screen by pressing 2nd [QUIT].
5. Clear the Home Screen by pressing CLEAR.

Patterns in logarithmic outputs

Refer to Figure 2.19 as you proceed through these steps:

1. To enter $\log(2^1)$, press

LOG († 2 ^ 1) ENTER.

†*This first parenthesis automatically appears on the TI-83.*

2. To enter $\log(2^2)$, press

2nd [ENTRY] ◄ ◄ 2 ENTER.

3. To enter $\log(2^3)$, press

2nd [ENTRY] ◄ ◄ 3 ENTER.

    See Figure 2.19. Do you see the pattern? A rule of logarithms states that for positive numbers x, $\log(x^n) = n \log(x)$. To see the pattern in a different way.

1. Press LOG 2nd [{] 2 , 4 , 8 2nd [}] ENTER, *adding parentheses if needed.*

2. Press and hold ► to see the third item in the "list." (See Fig. 2.20)

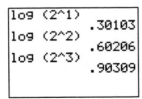

Figure 2.19

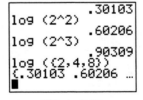

Figure 2.20

    The curly braces { } are used to enclose an ordered set of numbers, or **list.** List notation looks just like set notation, but you can add, subtract, multiply, and divide lists, whereas you operate on sets differently, using operations such as union and intersection. Your calculator manual has a chapter on lists. You also can learn about lists through experimentation; try using them in various ways and observe the results.

2.2.8   Using Variables

Example 3 Finding the Height of a Triangle

Problem A triangle encloses an area of 75 cm^2 and has a base of 11 cm. What is its height?

Solution   Recall that the area is given by one half the base times the height: $A = (1/2)bh$. Therefore to find the height, do the following:

1. To put your calculator in Floating Point mode,

   a. press $\boxed{\text{MODE}}$ and

   b. select the Float option.

2. Return to and clear the Home screen.

3. To store the value 11 as the variable B, press

   $$11 \;\boxed{\text{STO}\blacktriangleright}\; \boxed{\text{ALPHA}}\; \mathbf{B}\; \boxed{\text{ENTER}}.$$

4. Because one-half the base is about 5, the height should be about 15. Therefore press

   • on the TI-82,

   $$15 \;\boxed{\text{STO}\blacktriangleright}\; \boxed{\text{ALPHA}}\; \mathbf{H}\; \boxed{\text{2nd}}\; \boxed{:}\; \boxed{(}\; \mathbf{1}\; \boxed{\div}\; \mathbf{2}\; \boxed{)}\; \boxed{\text{2nd}}\; \boxed{\text{A-LOCK}}\; \mathbf{B}\; \mathbf{H}\; \boxed{\text{ENTER}}.$$

   • on the TI-83,

   $$15 \;\boxed{\text{STO}\blacktriangleright}\; \boxed{\text{ALPHA}}\; \mathbf{H}\; \boxed{\text{ALPHA}}\; \boxed{:}\; \boxed{(}\; \mathbf{1}\; \boxed{\div}\; \mathbf{2}\; \boxed{)}\; \boxed{\text{2nd}}\; \boxed{\text{A-LOCK}}\; \mathbf{B}\; \mathbf{H}\; \boxed{\text{ENTER}}.$$

   (See Fig. 2.21.)

5. Our guess was too big, so enter

   $$\boxed{\text{2nd}}\; \boxed{\text{ENTRY}}\; \boxed{\blacktriangle}\; \mathbf{14}\; \boxed{\text{ENTER}}.$$

   (See Fig. 2.22.)

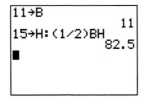

Figure 2.21

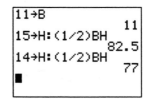

Figure 2.22

The next guess would be between 13 and 14 and would require inserting extra digits for the number being stored in H (press $\boxed{\text{2nd}}\;\boxed{\text{INS}}$ at the appropriate location). Continue the guess-and-check process to practice using the editing features of your calculator and to find the height with an error of no more than 0.01.

2.3   Function Graphing and Table Building

Graphing and table building on your calculator involve the top row of keys. There are four graphing modes on your calculator: Function, Parametric, Polar, and Sequence. Each has a corresponding table-building mode. Thus changing the setting on the fourth line of the Mode screen affects both graphing and table building (see Fig. 2.23).

(a)

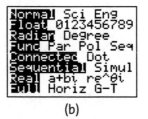

(b)

Figure 2.23   The Mode screen on the (a) TI-82 and (b) TI-83.

For this section, be sure your calculator is in Function mode (Func). In Section 2.4 we explore the Parametric and Polar modes. The remainder of this section is built around various calculator methods for solving equations, using the example

$$\cos x = \tan x \text{ for } 0 \le x \le 1.$$

2.3.1   Method A: Graphing Each Side and Zooming In

1. Enter each side of the equation as a function on the Y = screen by pressing

Insert parentheses if you wish to match Figure 2.24.

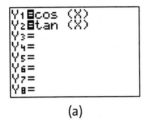   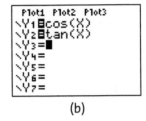

(a)   (b)

Figure 2.24 The Y = screen on the (a) TI-82 and (b) TI-83.

2. Press ZOOM [4 : ZDecimal].

Watch as the curves are graphed in sequence. The vertical lines are pseudoasymptotes of y = tan x. The calculator is actually connecting points that are off the screen (see Fig. 2.25).

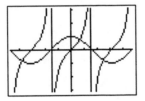

Figure 2.25

3. Press WINDOW to see what portion of the plane is being used for graphing. The viewing rectangle, or window, being used is [Xmin, Xmax] by [Ymin, Ymax], in this case [−4.7, 4.7] by [−3.1, 3.1]. Because Xscl = 1 and Yscl = 1, the tick marks on each axis are one unit apart (see Fig. 2.26). The TI-83 has an extra line on the Window screen to set the resolution. For our purposes, keep Xres = 1.

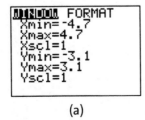   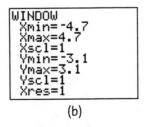

(a)   (b)

Figure 2.26 The Window editor screen on the (a) TI-82 and (b) TI-83.

4. Press TRACE

Observe the coordinate readout at the bottom of the screen as you press and release ▶ *repeatedly. Stop when x = 0.7. The graphs appear to intersect at x = 0.7; actually this is a rough approximation of the solution we seek for cos x = tan x for 0 ≤ x ≤ 1 (see Fig. 2.27).*

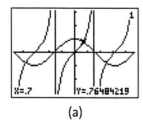
(a)

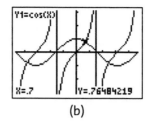
(b)

Figure 2.27 Tracing on the (a) TI-82 and (b) TI-83.

Now you can probably see why the fourth ZOOM feature is called Zoom Decimal (ZDecimal). It adjusted the viewing window to give a nice *decimal* readout. Notice the 1 in the upper right-hand corner of the TI-82 screen. It lets you know that you are tracing on Y_1, which in this case is cos x. The TI-83 shows the equation.

5. Press ⌐ ▼ ⌐ to move the Trace cursor to Y_2.

The x value does not change, but the y value does, because you are now tracing on Y_2 = tan x. Notice the screen indicator has changed to show you are tracing on Y_2 (see Fig. 2.28).

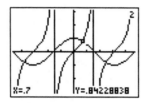

Figure 2.28 TI-82 version

6. Press ⌐GRAPH⌐.

The Trace cursor, the coordinate readout, and the number in the upper right-hand corner of the screen all disappear and only the graph itself is displayed (see Fig. 2.29).

7. Press any of the cursor-movement keys. You now are using a free-moving cursor that is not confined to either of the graphs. Notice that this cursor looks different from the Trace cursor.

8. Experiment with all four cursor-movement keys.

Watch the coordinate readout change. Move to the point (0.7, 0.8). Notice $y = 0.8$ is not the value of either function at $x = 0.7$, it is just the y-coordinate of a dot (pixel) on the graphing screen (see Fig. 2.30). The coordinates (0.7, 0.8) are the *screen coordinates* of the pixel. Notice that the free-moving cursor yields a nice decimal readout for both x and y. This is because we used Zoom Decimal to set the viewing window.

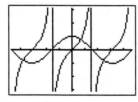

Figure 2.29

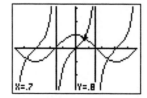

Figure 2.30

Using ZOOM Box. This option lets you use the cursor to select opposite corners of a "box" to define a new viewing window. Continuing the example from above, do the following:

1. Press ⌈ZOOM⌉ [1 : Box]. Then move the cursor to (0,0). (See Fig. 2.31.)

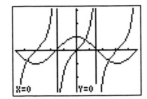

Figure 2.31

2. To select a new viewing window of [0, 1] by [0, 1.2], which will limit *x* so that

$$0 \leq x \leq 1,$$

   a. press ⌈ENTER⌉ to select the point (0, 0) as one corner of the new viewing window and

   b. use the cursor-movement keys to move to the opposite corner (1, 1.2). (See Fig. 2.32.)

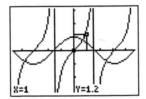

Figure 2.32

3. To select (1, 1.2) as the opposite corner of the new viewing window, press

⌈ENTER⌉.

The graphs of the two functions will be drawn in the new viewing window (see Fig. 2.33).

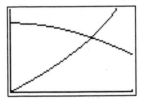

Figure 2.33

4. To remove the cursor and coordinates from the screen, press ⌈GRAPH⌉.

5. To verify that the new viewing rectangle is [0,1] by [0, 1.2], press ⌈WINDOW⌉.

Notice that Xscl and Yscl are still both equal to one. The Zoom Box option does not change the scale settings (see Fig. 2.34).

6. To approximate the solution as $x \approx 0.6702$,

   a. press ⌈TRACE⌉ and

   b. use the cursor-movement keys to move to the point of intersection (see Fig. 2.35).

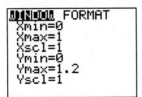

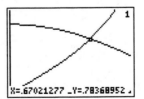

Figure 2.34 TI-82 version   **Figure 2.35** TI-82 version

Finding an error bound.   Next, using the approximate solution we found in number 6 above, we want to find the error bound for *x,* as follows:

1. To return to and clear the Home screen, press [2nd] [QUIT] [CLEAR].

2. To see the approximate solution, press ([X,T,θ]) [ENTER].

3. Press

   - on the TI-82 [VARS] [1 : Window] [7 : ΔX] [ENTER] or
   - on the TI-83 [VARS] [1 : Window] [8 : ΔX] [ENTER].

The value of Δx is the horizontal distance between consecutive pixels in the current viewing window, which in this case is about 0.011. This is an error bound for x. Our approximate solution 0.6702, has an error of at most 0.011.

   We need to pick Xmin and Xmax so that they are closer together to decrease this error bound (see Fig. 2.36).

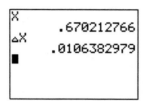

Figure 2.36

Do the following:

1. To enter the smaller window of [0.5, 0.8] by [0.6, 1.0], press [WINDOW], followed on the TI-82 by [▼]; then press

   0.5 [ENTER] **0.8** [ENTER] **0.1** [ENTER] **0.6** [ENTER] **1** [ENTER] **0.1** [ENTER].

   (See Fig. 2.37)

2. To move to the point of intersection—approximately (0.666, 0.786), press

   [TRACE]

   and then after the graph is drawn use the cursor-movement keys (see Fig. 2.38).

Figure 2.37 TI-82 version

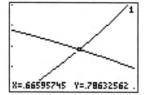

Figure 2.38 TI-82 version.

3. To display the previous approximation and error bound along with the new and improved approximation and error bound (see Fig. 2.39), press

   - on the TI-82 [2nd] [QUIT] [X,T,θ] [ENTER] [VARS] [1 : Window] [7 : ΔX] [ENTER].
   - on the TI-83 [2nd] [QUIT] [X,T,θ] [ENTER] [VARS] [1 : Window] [8 : ΔX] [ENTER].

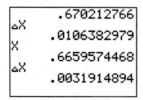

Figure 2.39

4. Evaluate cos x and tan x on your calculator. You should see the cos x and tan x are nearly, but not exactly, equal when $x = 0.6659...$ (see Fig. 2.40).

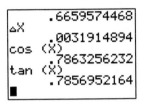

Figure 2.40

2.3.2 Method B: Table Building

The Y = screen is used to enter functions for both graphing and table building. To build a table, do as follows:

1. Press ⬚ Y= ⬚ to check that Y_1 = cos x and Y_2 = tan x (see Fig. 2.41).

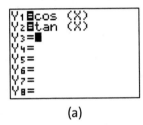   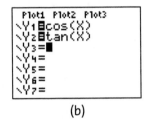

(a)   (b)

Figure 2.41 The Y = screen on the (a) TI-82 and (b) TI-83.

2. To reveal the Table Setup screen, press ⬚ 2nd ⬚ ⌊TBLSET⌋.

3. Press **0** ⌊ENTER⌋ **0.1** ⌊ENTER⌋ and ensure the Auto option is selected for both the independent variable (x) and the dependent variable (y) (see Fig. 2.42).

Figure 2.42

4. Press ⬚ 2nd ⬚ ⌊TABLE⌋ and notice that the first x-value is the TblMin (= 0) and that the increment from one row to the next in the x column is Δ Tbl (= 0.1) (see Fig. 2.43).

5. Press ⬚ ▼ ⬚ repeatedly to move down the x column of the table to 0.7. Notice that the solution lies between $x = 0.6$ and $x = 0.7$ (see Fig. 2.44).

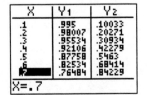

Figure 2.43   **Figure 2.44**

Use the cursor-movement keys to move around the table and explore. Pay attention to the readout at the bottom of the screen as you move to different cells in the table.

6. Press

2nd |TBLSET| **0.6** ENTER **0.01** ENTER.

The value of Δ Tbl will serve as the error bound for table building, just as Δx did for graphing (see Fig. 2.45).

7. Press 2nd |TABLE| and then press ▼ repeatedly until you reach $x = 0.67$. This is a solution with an error of at most 0.01 (see Fig. 2.46).

X	Y₁	Y₂
.61	.81965	.69892
.62	.81388	.71391
.63	.80803	.72911
.64	.8021	.74454
.65	.79608	.7602
.66	.78999	.7761
.67	.78382	.79225

X=.67

Figure 2.45   **Figure 2.46**

2.3.3 Method C: Solving an Equivalent Equation

To solve $\cos x = \tan x$ for $0 \le x \le 1$, you can solve the equivalent equation

$$\cos x - \tan x = 0$$

for the same interval. To do this on the TI-82, follow these steps:

1. Press

Y= ▼ ▼ 2nd |Y-VARS|† [1 : Function...] [1 : Y₁] — 2nd

|Y-VARS|† [1 : Function...] [2 : Y₂] ENTER

†On the TI-83, use VARS ▶ in place of 2nd |Y-VARS|.

(See Fig. 2.47).

2. To deselect Y₁ and Y₂, press

▲ ▲ ◀ ENTER ▲ ENTER.

Now only Y₃ should have its equals sign highlighted (see Fig. 2.48).

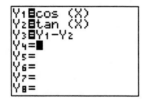

Figure 2.47 TI-82 version.   **Figure 2.48** TI-82 version.

3. To see the graph of $y = \cos x - \tan x$ in a friendly viewing window, press

ZOOM [4 : ZDecimal]; and after the graph is drawn, press

TRACE 2nd ▶ ▶ ▶.

Notice 2nd ▶ *moves the cursor five pixels to the right for fast tracing (see Fig. 2.49).*

4. To enter the Zoom Factors screen, press

ZOOM ▶ [4 : SetFactors...]

and enter 10 as both the horizontal and the vertical magnification factor by pressing

10 ENTER **10** ENTER.

(See Fig 2.50.)

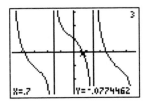

Figure 2.49 TI-82 version.

Figure 2.50

5. To center your zoom-in at the point $(x, y) = (0.7, 0)$, press

[ZOOM] [2 : ZoomIn]

and move the cursor to $(0.7, 0)$. (See Fig. 2.51.)

Then press [ENTER] to zoom in.

6. After the graph is redrawn, you can obtain the same approximation that was found by Method B by pressing

[TRACE] [◄] [◄] [◄].

Check the value of Δx; it is the same as the Δ Tbl in method B! (See Fig. 2.52.)

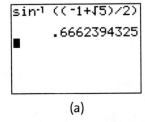

Figure 2.51 TI-82 version.

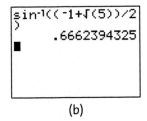

Figure 2.52

2.3.4   Other Equation-Solving Methods

Traditional algebra and trigonometry can be used to determine the exact solution of equation 1.

$$x = \sin^{-1}\frac{-1 + \sqrt{5}}{2}$$

Do the following:

1. To evaluate this expression on your calculator, enter it as shown in Figure 2.53.

You obtain an approximation that is accurate to 10 decimal places. It should be consistent with those found by Methods A, B, and C, and it is (see Fig. 2.53).

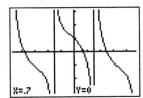
(a)

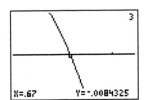
(b)

Figure 2.53 An arcsin computation on the (a) TI-82 and (b) TI-83

2. Set up your Y = screen as you did for Method C. Then, to obtain a graph, press

[ZOOM] [4 : ZDecimal].

3. Press [2nd] [CALC] [2 : root]. (On the TI-83, the word "zero" appears rather than "root.") *This should yield a prompt requesting a Lower Bound or Left Bound (see Fig. 2.54).*

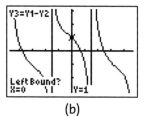

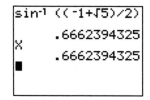

Figure 2.54 (a) Root finder on the TI-82, (b) zero finder on the TI-83.

4. Because we are seeking a solution for $0 \leq x \leq 1$, the lower bound should be $x = 0$; so press ENTER.

5. To move the cursor to $x = 1$, press

   followed by ENTER to enter it as the upper bound.

6. Move the Trace cursor to $x = 0.7$ and enter it as your guess by pressing

The calculator should yield a root value of $x = 0.66623943$ (see Fig. 2.55).

7. To compare the value found using the root finder and the value found in Part 1 above, press

   X,T,θ ENTER.

They match perfectly to 10 decimal places! (See fig. 2.56.)

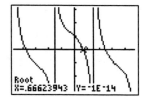

Figure 2.55 TI-82 version.

Figure 2.56 TI-82 version.

There are many other ways to solve equations on your calculator. Feel free to explore them.

2.4 Other Graphing and Table Building

2.4.1 Parametric Graphing and Table Building

Parametric equations are ideal tools for representing and solving problems in geometry and the physics of motion. Your calculator has a built-in parametric graphing utility. This utility is similar to the function graphing utility and is almost as easy to use. To graph a parametric curve, you

- select the parametric (Par) mode on the Mode screen.
- type the desired equations in the Y= screen,
- set the intervals for t, x, and y using the Window screen, and
- press GRAPH.

   Parametric equations are written in the form:

$$x = f(t) \text{ and } y = g(t).$$

In this setting t is called a parameter; however, t actually is an independent variable, not a parameter in the sense that m and b are parameters in the equation $y = mx + b$. Unlike the independent variable x we are used to in Function-graphing mode, the parameter t is not a plotted, visible coordinate; it is hidden from view when we look at a parametric curve. When we use the TRACE feature, we see a readout of the parameter t and the coordinates x and y, which are the dependent variables of the parametric representation.

Example 4   Graphing a Parametric Curve

Problem Graph the curve represented by the following parametric equations:

$$x = t^2 \text{ and } y = t - 1 \text{ for } -2 \leq t \leq 2.$$

Solution To solve this problem, follow these steps:

1. Press [MODE] to enter the Mode screen and

   a. select Parametric Graphing (Par) and

   b. choose the default (leftmost) settings for the other mode settings.

2. Because we are in Parametric mode, pressing [X,T,θ] will yield the letter t. To enter the given parametric equations, press

   [Y=] [X,T,θ] [x^2] [ENTER] [X,T,θ] [−] **1** [ENTER].

The screen should look like Figure 2.57.

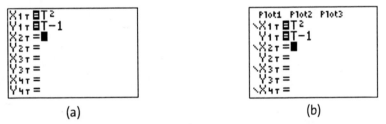

(a)	(b)

Figure 2.57 The Y= screen on the (a) TI-82 and (b) TI-83.

3. Press [WINDOW] and then set the Window screen as shown in Figure 2.58. (Note that you won't be able to see the entire screen at once because it has too many lines.)

Figure 2.58 Facsimile of the Window screen.

The t step on the Parametric Window screen is the change between the successive t-values that the calculator uses to compute and plot (x, y) pairs. In this case, the t step of 0.1 will yield 40 steps from the t Min of -2 to the t Max of 2. Thus 41 points will be calculated and plotted, with the points corresponding to

$$t = -2.0, -1.9, -1.8, -1.7, \ldots, 1.9, 2.0.$$

Table 2.3 shows the numerical relationship between the parameter t and the coordinates x and y for some of the points to be plotted.

The last two columns of Table 2.3 determine the (x, y) coordinate pairs to be plotted. The values of the parameter t will not appear on the graph.

You can create a table like Table 2.3 on your calculator as follows:

1. Press 2nd |TBLSET| (−) 2 ENTER 0.1 ENTER. (See Fig. 2.59.)
2. Then press 2nd |TABLE|. (See Fig. 2.60.)

Table 2.3 Table of Parameter and Coordinate Values

t	$x = t^2$	$y = t - 1$
−2.0	4.00	−3.0
−1.9	3.61	−2.9
−1.8	3.24	−2.8
−1.7	2.89	−2.7
.	.	.
.	.	.
.	.	.
1.9	3.61	0.9
2.0	4.00	1.0

Figure 2.59

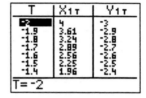

Figure 2.60

To obtain the graph corresponding to Table 2.3 and Figure 2.60, do the following:

1. Press GRAPH to yield the plot shown in Figure 2.61.

Because the calculator is in Connected mode, the plotted points in Figure 2.61 are connected by the line segments.

2. To display only the 41 plotted points, choose the Dot mode from the Mode screen and press GRAPH again (see Fig. 2.62).

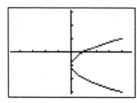

Figure 2.61

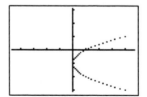

Figure 2.62

Return to Connected mode and use the TRACE feature and the left and right cursor-movement keys to explore the graph numerically. Notice that the values of the parameter t and the x- and y-coordinates are all shown on the screen (see Fig. 2.63 and 2.64). Can you find the six points that correspond to the completed rows of Table 2.3?

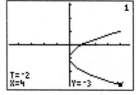

Figure 2.63 TI-82 version.

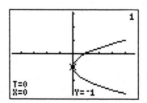

Figure 2.64 TI-82 version.

2.4.2   Polar Equation Graphing

The Polar Equation graphing mode is similar to the other graphing modes.

Example 5   Graphing Two Equations Simultaneously

Problem   Graph $r = 9 \sin 5\theta$ and $r = 9$.
Solution

1. Press $\boxed{\text{MODE}}$ (see Fig. 2.65) and

   a. select Polar (Pol) mode and Simultaneous (Simul) mode and

   b. choose the defaults for the other modes.

2. Press $\boxed{\text{Y=}}$ to display the Polar Equation screen.

3. To define the two desired equations, press

$$\mathbf{9} \boxed{\text{SIN}} \mathbf{5} \boxed{\text{X,T,}\theta} \boxed{\text{ENTER}} \mathbf{9} \boxed{\text{ENTER}}.$$

(See Fig. 2.66.)

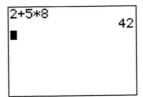

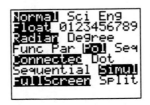

Figure 2.65 TI-82 version.

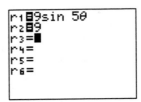

Figure 2.66 TI-82 version.

4. Press $\boxed{\text{ZOOM}}$ [6 : ZStandard].

The graph of $r = 9$ is a circle of radius 9 centered at the pole. The circle circumscribes the five-petaled rose curve $r = 9 \sin 5\theta$ (see Fig. 2.67).

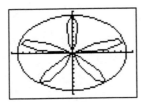

Figure 2.67

5. Set θmax $= \pi$ in the Window screen.

6. To "square up" the window, press

[ZOOM] [5 : ZSquare].

The entire rose curve is plotted using the interval $0 \le \theta \le \pi$. *Press* [TRACE] *and explore the two curves (see Fig. 2.68).*

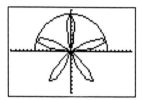

Figure 2.68